PERSIAN CATS
KW-061

Contents

Photographers: Jack T. Arneson, Tom Caravaglia, CLI, Isabelle Francais, Dorothy Holby, Fritz Prenzel, Purina Pet Care Center, Ron Reagan, Vincent Serbin, Skotzke and Lucas, Sally Anne Thompson, Louise van der Meid.

Title page: *The beautiful long, flowing coat and large, brilliant eyes of the Persian, together with its gentle disposition, make this an especially popular breed among cat fanciers.*

Distributed in the UNITED STATES by T.F.H. Publications, Inc., One T.F.H. Plaza, Neptune City, NJ 07753; in CANADA to the Pet Trade by H & L Pet Supplies Inc., 27 Kingston Crescent, Kitchener, Ontario N2B 2T6; Rolf C. Hagen Ltd., 3225 Sartelon Street, Montreal 382 Quebec; in CANADA to the Book Trade by Macmillan of Canada (A Division of Canada Publishing Corporation), 164 Commander Boulevard, Agincourt, Ontario M1S 3C7; in ENGLAND by T.F.H. Publications Limited, Cliveden House/Priors Way/Bray, Maidenhead, Berkshire SL6 2HP, England; in AUSTRALIA AND THE SOUTH PACIFIC by T.F.H. (Australia) Pty. Ltd., Box 149, Brookvale 2100 N.S.W., Australia; in NEW ZEALAND by Ross Haines & Son, Ltd., 18 Monmouth Street, Grey Lynn, Auckland 2, New Zealand; in SINGAPORE AND MALAYSIA by MPH Distributors (S) Pte., Ltd., 601 Sims Drive, #03/07/21, Singapore 1438; in the PHILIPPINES by Bio-Research, 5 Lippay Street, San Lorenzo Village, Makati Rizal; in SOUTH AFRICA by Multipet Pty. Ltd., 30 Turners Avenue, Durban 4001. Published by T.F.H. Publications, Inc. Manufactured in the United States of America by T.F.H. Publications, Inc.

PERSIAN CATS

BY EDWARD E. ESARDE

Left: *The Persian head is round, massive, and well set on a short, thick neck. The ears are small and set far apart; the nose, short and snub with a break (indentation).*
Below: *Some experts believe that the delicate, silky texture of the Persian coat can be attributed to a Persian-Angora cross.*

A Portrait of the

Persian Cat

The Persian Cat is surely the most elegant of all cats. Its distinctive long, glossy coat, large jewel-like eyes, small ears, full-brush tail and sweet facial expression have caused it to rank among the most preferred of all purebred cats. Careful breeding by cat fanciers over the last one hundred years has greatly refined the appearance of the Persian into the form we know today, but the animal's aristocratic mannerisms remain basically unchanged.

Longhaired cats existed

long before the Persian as it is known today. What the Persian is noted for, however, is its plush, thick, double coat; other breeds now having this double coat may thank the Persian, though a Persian-Angora cross may have been responsible for the long, fine, silky-textured coat and the compliant, tractable manner of today's Persian. The Angora is a recognized breed of cat accepted in all major Cat Fancy organizations in the United States and Canada and is accepted for Championship status. It is classified as a "natural" breed, and its re-establishment in the Cat Fancy in the United States and Canada is credited to Colonel Walter Grant, United States Army. Colonel Grant imported a pair of white Angoras from the Ata Turk Zoo, Ankara, Turkey, in 1962. A second pair was imported by him in 1966. Since the import

of these first pairs, many breeders have imported additional cats from Ankara and are breeding them for competition in United States and Canadian shows.

The Persian is a sturdy cat with a heavy bone structure. Its head is round and massive and sits sturdily on broad shoulders. The Persian's most pronounced feature is its long, flowing coat. The thick mane, or "ruff," which surrounds its neck gives the Persian the regal attitude of a lion.

The temperament of the Persian is certainly not that of a lion. The Persian is truly a *domesticated* cat. It loves to be with people and to show affection to those who love it. It is docile and sweet, yet it carries an air of respectability. It would

Facing: *A beautiful white Persian kitten from the Allaborde Cattery.*

Persians are bred in a great variety of colors, including solids, bicolors, and particolors. **Left:** A cream Persian kitten. **Below:** The beautiful "ruff" surrounding the neck of this gleaming white Persian is comparable to the mane of a lion. **Facing:** A shaded silver Persian.

The beauty and elegance of the Persian give the breed the regal bearing which is respected and loved by fanciers around the world.

seem to prefer a comfortable life of lounging around indoors to a life that pits it against the elements of the wilderness. All in all, the Persian is certainly among the most regal of all the breeds that represent *Felis domesticus.*

ANCIENT ANCESTRY

Though the exact origin of the breed will probably never be proved, many authorities believe that the first ancestors of the Persian came from the area of the Kingdom of Persia (now Iran) and Turkey. Most experts agree that the Persian was mated to a longhair from the Middle East; some say Afghanistan, and others credit this cat's native habitat to be Russia. This Russian cat was green-eyed and had a coat of beige ground color marked with indistinct, very smeared, tabby markings. It was used in conjunction with the Turkish Angora to breed to the Persian, producing today's long, flowing, double coat. *Note:* The Persian is credited with introducing the double coat, and the Turkish Angora is credited with providing the long, flowing coat. Over the years, selective breeding of the Persian has developed the Persian coat to the beauty it has today.

Headstudy of a Chinchilla kitten. Note the sweet expression on its face.

Today, the Persian cat continues to flourish as a breed. Thousands of pedigrees are registered with the various distinguished organizations of cat fanciers. Family trees are recorded in registries that outline the Persian lineage back through many generations. Yes, the Persian is truly among the social elite of catdom.

THE FORMAL PERSIAN

The various cat associations have set forth their Standards of Perfection that define the "perfect" cat for which all breeders strive. The

perfect cat has a total possible score of 100 points . . . a level never achieved by a breeder. The use of these Standards aids a judge in selecting those cats that "come the closest" to perfection. Such cats are awarded ribbons (points) which are then credited towards the titles of "Champion," and the ultimate in the Cat Fancy, Grand Champion. Persian kittens that least meet the established standards are not likely to be used as breeding stock by finer catteries.

Selecting a Persian

WHERE TO FIND A PERSIAN KITTEN

Persian kittens may be found for sale at your local pet shop, through newspaper ads or directly from a cattery. Your veterinarian may be able to suggest a pet shop or cattery in your area. The making of fine pedigreed Persian cats is not an accident of nature. The most beautiful Persian cats are the result of a great deal of thought and planning. Special care is taken in selecting the proper sire and dam for the characteristics of coat color, texture and length, shape of the head and body, eyes, over-all form, personality and good health. All the standards of the breed are taken into consideration when the mating of two purebred Persians is planned by a responsible breeder.

If you are planning to show your Persian cat and you have never shown before, it is a good idea to attend several cat shows before buying a kitten. That way you can make your purchase with a better understanding of the standards observed by the various cat organizations. You may also gain important information concerning the value of different pedigrees or family lines and about where to find experienced breeders. A good reputation travels by word of mouth. It takes an experienced cat fancier to distinguish between the show and pet types of Persians, so in many cases the buyer may be forced to rely on the reputation of the breeder. Some catteries will sell their best potential show cats only to people who will enter them in competition at cat shows.

The price of a Persian will vary considerably depending on the pedigree, the showing potential of the kitten and where you buy it. Other

Many purebred kittens have small flaws that are noticeable only to experienced breeders who are familiar with the breed standard. These kittens make wonderful pets and are often available.

The purchase of a healthy *kitten* cannot be overemphasized. Before making your final selection, take a few minutes to observe the kitten you are interested in buying. **Left and below:** *Kittens are naturally curious. Look for an alert and active kitten, one that is aware of its surroundings.* **Facing:** *A healthy kitten's eyes should be clear and free of foreign matter; the coat should be clean, thick, and glossy; the nose should not be runny.*

variables such as economic conditions and geographic location also must be considered.

If you decide to obtain a purebred kitten solely to have as a pet, you can usually purchase the kitten for much less than a breeder- or show-type kitten. In this case the breeder may wish to "hold" the pedigree papers until after the kitten has been spayed or neutered.

Whether you intend to show or not, there are several advantages to buying a purebred kitten. First, by observing the kitten's sire and dam, you can gain an idea of what the kitten will be like as an adult. Secondly, a purebred Persian is a cat that has been bred purposely for its traits as both a show cat and a house pet. Lastly, your animal has an aristocratic heritage that can be traced to four or more generations.

SELECTING A HEALTHY KITTEN

It is very important, when choosing your Persian kitten, that you find one that is healthy. A healthy kitten will make a better pet and a better show animal, and it will save you money in extra trips to the veterinarian. First, observe the kitten to see if it is alert and well aware of its surroundings; it should respond to different stimuli of sight and sound. Test the kitten's hearing by creeping up behind it and clapping your hands. The kitten should be easily startled and will probably jump in the air. Test the kitten's sight by observing if it will play with a ball or other toy placed in front of it. Kittens are naturally curious, but some are more inquisitive than others. Just as people are not equally intelligent, the same is true for cats.

If possible, compare the various kittens in the litter. Are they all fairly fit and

Double Champion Dulcie Jean's Sphiro of Geris, a black male. Owned by Geri Hamilton, Bricktown, NJ.

Top left: *Kittens love to play, especially outdoors; however, because they are so inquisitive, sometimes they get themselves into dangerous situations. This white kitten is trying to climb up on a ledge where it doesn't belong.* **Top right and above:** *It is best to keep your new Persian indoors and to divert its attention with some good, safe toys such as this small rubber ball.* **Facing:** *Your Persian kitten must learn what is "off limits" in its new home. A sharp clap of the hands, accompanied by a firm "no!" is most effective. Consistency, however, is the key.*

active? What is their environment like? Cats raised under good conditions are more likely to have healthy kittens. Try not to fall in love with the runt of the litter if there is one. It may have a serious congenital illness or other potential health problems. Look for a kitten with a good sturdy frame and some meat on its bones. The eyes should be clear and free from irritation, tearing or discharge. The kitten should be breathing easily and should have no nasal discharge. A sneezing kitten with a runny nose and runny eyes may have a serious respiratory problem, which could make things miserable for it and for you in the future. Check the gums; they should be firm and pink and free of sores. The skin should be free of rashes. The coat should be

Kittens allowed to play outdoors should be supervised at all times.

Keystone Juniper, owned by Marianne Lawrence, Insta-Purr Cattery, Jackson, NJ.

Left: *Persians that are allowed to roam outdoors run the risk of getting their long, flowing coats tangled and dirty. They also have a greater chance of getting hit by a car or of getting into fights with other cats. For these reasons, it is best to keep your Persian indoors.* **Below and facing:** *Your Persian can peacefully coexist with other felines or other pets as long as all parties are properly introduced.*

glossy and soft and without bare patches. A kitten with a generally unthrifty appearance may be less expensive to buy initially, but it is likely to cost you much more in veterinary bills. If you have any doubts about the health of a kitten you're thinking of obtaining, have the kitten examined by your veterinarian *before* you acquire it. Also, the

kitten you plan to purchase should have its shots (and time to become immune) prior to leaving for a new home.

If you purchase your kitten from a litter, do not take your kitten home and away from its mother until it has been fully weaned. Depending on Mother Nature, this could be anywhere from 2-3 months. By this time, a kitten should be trained (by its mother) to use the litter box, and it will have increased strength and stamina to adjust to its new surroundings. When you first bring the kitten home, give it time to investigate its new domain and avoid excessive handling at first. Your kitten will soon make your home its home.

MALE OR FEMALE?
Aside from the obvious physical differences between male and female cats, there are several behavioral differences that

Kittens love to play hide-and-seek; therefore, a watchful eye is a necessity.

A grave outdoor hazard is the presence of poisonous plants. Kittens should never be permitted to eat any type of flora.

he buyer may wish to consider. For example, although female cats are in general more affectionate than males, individual females may be more cautious about approaching and getting comfortable with a new owner or house guest than a male cat. As a potential mother, the female may instinctively be more concerned or threatened by possible changes in her environment. Once you are adopted by your female cat, however, she generally

will be more affectionate and loving than a male. She will become very content and even possessive of you and her surroundings. Male cats, on the other hand—even those that may tend to be more affectionate at first with both a new owner and even strangers—are, in the main, more aloof than females. Some males may jump into your lap the minute they see you, and, in their own obvious way, request that you give them the standard rubdown. With this same sort of confidence, a male cat may also wish to explore a little farther away from home than a female. The male cat also will tend to be a little larger than the female and often is more

rash, boisterous and aggressive.

You will find that the sexual life of adult cats may take strong preference over their other interests. The mature, non- neutered male cat that is confined in the house and unable to mate with a female will in time become increasingly restless and irritable. He will pace unhappily around the

house waiting only for a chance to leave home; your tom (non-neutered male) may be unable to eat or sleep and will have no time to play or to be affectionate. Most toms will "spray" or urinate on furniture and walls in an instinctive attempt to mark their territory and to attract females. If you allow your non-neutered male cat to roam outside, he is likely to get into numerous fights with other stray cats, and he is also at an increased risk of being hit by a car. If you are not planning to breed or show your male cat, the best way to alleviate his anxiety and eliminate his desire to roam and to "spray" is to have him neutered. Neutering the male cat is a simple and fairly inexpensive operation and is most effective in preventing the tom cat behavior if it is performed while the cat is young. The neutered male cat is generally much more

affectionate, playful and considerate of its surroundings.

The intact (non-spayed) female cat, or queen, when in heat will suffer the same sexual anxiety as the male cat. When in heat, the female cat will vocalize constantly. She may roll on her back as if dizzy, and she may "spray" in a manner similar to that of the male cat. Most important, if the female is allowed to roam, she runs the risk of becoming pregnant and having kittens. Additionally, it should be noted that continued "seasons" (heat cycles) without breeding can affect the health of a cat; cystic ovaries and other maladies that can lead to serious problems and expensive medical treatment can occur. So, if you are not interested in breeding your female Persian, you may wish to consider having her spayed. As with the male cat, the spayed female is

When two kittens are raised together, they form a bond similar to that of siblings.
They will keep each other busy and will usually keep each other out of trouble.

relieved of her sexual frustration and will become a much more affectionate and playful house pet.

Though male and female Persians may differ slightly in their personalities, both make equally wonderful pets. It is best to choose the one that fits your personality and lifestyle. Every year your cat matures, he or she will grow in intelligence and personality to give you continuing delight.

TWO CATS ARE TWICE AS MUCH FUN

If you are considering the purchase of a Persian kitten, why not think about getting two? I have found that it is true that two cats are twice as much fun and only half the worry. If you are away from home during the day or don't have a great deal of time to devote to them, two kittens will play together constantly and will grow in personality in leaps and bounds . . . literally. Just as any child will become

bored and get into mischief if left alone, so will a kitten. When two kittens are raised together they form an inseparable bond. They will sleep together and play together all day and night, and as they grow, their personalities will become more individualized and delightful than ever.

If you already have an adult cat and would like to bring home another kitten, it is fine to do so. You should, however, be prepared for a short period of adjustment. Some older cats will immediately accept a young kitten and even adopt it as its own, while other cats may feel slightly threatened, even to the point of becoming aggressive towards the kitten. Both of these reactions are perfectly natural. It is most important for you as the instigator of this new relationship to be patient while the two new acquaintances get to know

These adorable gray kittens enjoy pushing each other in their wagon. Kittens can be remarkably creative in their playtime activities.

one another. Although fighting is unlikely, in the case of an older cat and a new kitten, it is often wise to clip their claws before putting them together. This way, if they do decide to tangle, they are both less likely to get hurt. To start the relationship off

The kitten on the right is a Persian, while the kitten on the left is a Himalayan. Himalayans are a breed created by a cross between Persian and Siamese cats. Persian crosses have resulted in the creation of a number of new breeds.

correctly it is best to introduce the new kitten to your cat. Let them feel each other out. They will sniff one another and may spit and hiss as they establish an order of dominance. They may even play at first, or they may end up in a scuffle. Cats will usually end up in a stand-off, with the older cat establishing its dominance. Once again, this is perfectly natural and should be allowed to occur without interference. Your older cat may demand and need a bit more attention and affection for awhile to help alleviate its jealousy of its new "rival." Eventually, however, both cats will become comfortable with the new arrangement, and harmony will be restored. The new relationship will grow without malice; a true friendship will eventually ensue.

A good program to follow in introducing a kitten to an older cat already in your home would be to put the older cat in a closed room and let the kitten loose to explore and learn where the food and litter box are. After an hour or two at a minimum, formally introduce the two cats to each other. Let them see each other and smell each other, but hold the older cat during the process. Then let the older cat go. Speak softly and reassure both animals. It usually takes about a week for the cats to adjust to one another. If the cats don't get along even after a get-together period of two weeks, you might have a permanently incompatible pair on your hands—in which case the fairest thing to do is to try to return the younger cat to the person from whom you acquired it or to try to find it a good new home.

Living with a Persian Cat

Persian cats are particularly suited for the indoor life. Once they are accustomed to their new home, they will be perfectly content.

Of all the different types of house pets, the cat is probably the easiest with which to live. It can thrive in rural, suburban and urban environments. Cats love the outdoors, yet they are also extremely content to live their entire lives indoors. Indeed, the cat almost seems born for the indoor life. Persian cats, especially, have been bred over the centuries for the

Facing: *An adorable kitten owned by Jose Langevin.*

indoor life. Though they may carry an air of independence, Persian cats are generally docile and loving and need someone to care for them.

MAKING FRIENDS

Get to be your Persian cat's best friend. Take time to get acquainted. When you first bring your Persian kitten home, give it some time to investigate and become accustomed to its new surroundings. Don't initially smother it with constant cuddling and affection. If you pick the kitten up all the time and hold it against its will, it will want to avoid you in the future. Try not to force yourself on your new cat. Approach the kitten slowly until it gets to know you. Talk to it gently when it is relaxed. Stroke it gently and find out where it likes to be petted. You cannot force a friendship with a cat; you must *earn* the cat's friendship by gaining its respect. By feeding it

regularly, keeping the litter box clean, grooming your pet, talking to it and giving it a warm, dry place to sleep, you will gain a friend for life. Your cat will return the affection, keep you entertained constantly and fill you with wonderment and joy.

INSIDE OR OUTSIDE?

Although cats by instinct are hunters and explorers, the Persian cat is especially well adapted to living indoors. Its docile and affectionate manner has made it a superior house pet. The Persian is a superbly clean and neat animal. It stays clean by licking itself before, after, and during meals, and even during playtime. Regular daily grooming and brushing of the coat will prevent excessive shedding of hair onto your furniture and carpet. (More importantly, however, grooming and brushing is the best prevention for ensuring your cat does not

Champion Reimar's Puzzles of Insta-Purr, a blue cream Persian. Owned by Marianne Lawrence, Insta-Purr Cattery.

have problems with "hairballs." Persians continually groom themselves, but all of the loose hairs are ingested and create hairballs which can lead to medical problems and expense for owners, along with discomfort for the cat. The cat that is kept indoors all the time can be as happy as any cat that is free to roam. This confinement indoors, however, should not be such that it denies the cat the freedom to exercise and play. Climbing posts and playtoys, available in most pet shops, will supply endless amusement for the indoor cat.

If you are planning to allow your Persian to roam freely outdoors, there are several things that you should consider. First of all, most cities and towns and even some counties have ordinances prohibiting the free roaming of cats. If your cat is picked up by the local authorities, you may be required to pay a fine to get it back. Secondly, though many cats will readily find their way home in time for their dinner, some will decide to stay out for the evening, or two evenings, or you may not see your cat for a week. Free-roaming cats are likely to get into numerous fights with other cats, and are in danger of being hit by a car. In some cases, your cat may wander too far from home, and you may never see it again. A third consideration is your Persian's long coat. Persians that are allowed to roam outdoors will get excessive matting and tangling of their fur. To remove these tangles will require much time and patience in grooming and will be irritating and painful to your cat.

If you do not wish to keep your cat indoors but do not want it to roam, there are many types of outdoor housing that can

Kittens, in particular, are in danger of losing fights to other cats if they are allowed to roam at will. **Below:** *Allaborde's Amber enjoying a supervised outing.*

be used. Outdoor cat accommodations should be well ventilated but designed to protect your cat from drafts, rain, heat and cold. These accommodations should be large enough to allow the animal adequate room for exercise and play. Some well-designed cat houses have two or even three levels which allow the cat to jump and climb. Your cat's house should be kept clean and dry at all times. It should contain a comfortable sleeping place such as a basket or a box with a washable blanket, food dishes and, of course, a litter box which should be cleaned regularly.

THE LITTER BOX

An essential piece of equipment for every cat owner is the litter box or pan. Cats are instinctively clean animals and take scrupulous care in covering up their droppings with litter or dirt. It is the owner's duty to keep his or her cat's litter box clean.

There are several excellent commercially manufactured litter pans which are available at your local pet store. I recommend the plastic litter pans because they are so easy to clean. Be sure the litter pan is large enough for your cat (or cats) and that it is of sturdy construction. Some commercially produced litter pans provide a "double bottom" that leaves airspace for circulation under the litter; thus, the litter stays dry and odors are reduced. These pans are excellent for the one or two cat home, and they also extend the life of the litter (which may save money in the long run).

The pan should be filled with a commercially prepared cat litter. Most commercially available brands of cat litter are

A beautiful example of the odd-eyed white variety of Persians.

made of absorbent granulated clay or a similar material. These commercial brands are usually fairly inexpensive and are by far the most effective for controlling wetness and odor. With Persians, there are two cautions regarding the selection of litter. First, do not use a sawdust or pressed pulp wood type litter. This light material will get caught in the cat's coat and cause matting and extra grooming for the owner. Secondly, if you have a white or lightly colored cat, beware of "colored" litter. Certain litters that have been treated with additives to reduce odor may cause staining on your Persian's paws and lower leg hair.

A common problem encountered at one time or another by all cat fanciers is an offensive litter box odor. The best way to control the odor of your cat's litter box is to clean it regularly. You will find that your cat will appreciate this as much as you will. A cat is very unhappy when its litter box is too dirty, and it may express its dissatisfaction by leaving droppings in less appropriate places. Another good hint to control litter box odor is to sprinkle a little baking soda in the bottom of the pan before adding the litter. Special products are now available to help control smell, and, some litters have special additives to help control odor.

If your cat insists on flinging the litter out of the box or neatly wiping the litter off the edge of the box and onto the floor, it may help to set the plastic litter pan in a larger cardboard box with higher walls. If the walls are too high, a doorway can be cut in one side of the cardboard box to allow the cat free entry to the litter pan.

The importance of a clean litter pan cannot be

A clean cat is a happy cat. Cats are neat by nature, but they need help to maintain their beautiful coat. Persians, with their long hair, are especially in need of good grooming.

overemphasized. The droppings should be removed from the litter box at least once a day. Commercially available plastic shovels are ideal for this task. At least once a week, or more often if necessary (depending on how many cats use the box), the dirty litter should be disposed of and the litter pan should be cleaned thoroughly with soap and water. Fresh new litter should be placed into the pan after each cleaning, and it's a good idea to dry the pan thoroughly before putting in the new litter; if the pan is wet, the litter granules can stick together.

TRAINING

Cats that are properly raised with their mother, and that are sufficiently weaned and ready to leave home, normally will be trained to the litter pan. A mother cat is the world's best teacher on the use of a litter pan and cleanliness. All of this seems to come very naturally to kittens, since cats instinctively prefer to scratch a hole and neatly bury their excretions. Should you happen to purchase a kitten that is *not* litter box trained, it is best to keep the litter box close to where the kitten sleeps and eats. After the kitten has eaten a meal, pick it up and stand it down in the litter box. It may just dig and play at first, but you will be amazed at how fast it will take to using the litter box on its own. Be sure that the sides of the litter box are not so high that they prevent easy access. If you have a spacious home and your kitten is allowed to roam a larger area, it is a good idea to have two litter boxes so that your kitten will not have as far to travel when it feels the need to go to the "bathroom." Once a cat has adjusted to a litter pan in one specific place, you

Every kitten should have a place of its own. There are many kinds of cat beds available at pet shops, and the basket-type beds are especially attractive.

should attempt to keep that location. A cat finding the normal place for the litter pan empty of the needed pan may find the carpet, and still lingering odors of the missing litter pan, a good substitute.

Cats can, and should, be trained to know their name. Before feeding your cat, you should call its name several times in a clear, distinctive tone. It may also help to use a higher than normal pitch in your voice. Use the cat's name frequently in play and it will eventually know who it is. Your Persian may not come every time it's called, but when it does, you should reward it with affection—and perhaps a small food treat.

As for training cats to perform any complex tasks, cats would like to have us believe that this is totally out of the question.

Cats are very intelligent animals and can learn very quickly. They can also pretend to have forgotten what was taught when they so desire.

Scratching posts are a necessity, as cats will instinctively scratch furniture when not provided with such a post.

Cats may be fully attentive one minute but will be off in a complete world of their own the next.

Training the cat requires love, patience, and consistency. The more affection you show your cat, the more personality it will attain. Every cat is a delightful individual that is waiting to be discovered. The cat's intelligence will surprise you at every turn.

SCRATCHING THE FURNITURE

Cats love to stretch out their front legs and scratch and knead with their paws. This is a natural form of exercise and is an indication of contentment for most cats, but it can be very hard on the walls, furniture and carpets. Supplying your cat with a scratching post should help alleviate this problem.

A scratching post can be a source of endless enjoyment for your kitten or cat, provided the post is fastened securely to the floor or walls so as not to tip over. Our cats will scale their scratching post as if it were a real tree and perform incredible acrobatics on it. It will also save on furniture and carpets if you clip your cat's claws regularly. But be very careful not to clip too short. If your cat persists in scratching on all the wrong pieces of furniture and is destroying the carpet and walls, you may wish to contact your veterinarian to discuss the pros and cons of declawing. Declawing, however, should be only a last-resort solution—it is much better to provide a proper scratching post and to train the cat in its use.

HARNESS AND LEASH

If you are planning to take your Persian cat out for walks, it should be trained to a harness and leash. For Persian cats, the "figure 8" style harness seems to work the best. Regular collars can be slipped off over the head and will cause excessive matting and tearing of the fur around the mane. The "figure 8" harness is easy to put on and will stay on securely during walks. Since the harness goes under the front legs and belly and over the shoulders, there is more control and restraint and less risk of the cat's being choked by a collar.

Becoming accustomed to a harness and leash may require a bit of practice until your cat gets used to it. At first your cat will want to roll on its back and play with the leash. It will find the entire idea very amusing. Eventually, however, it will tire of the game and begin to take the leash more seriously.

A beautiful male cream Persian.

PLAYTIME, TOYS AND A BASKET

Playing comes naturally to the cat. Persians, like all other cats, love and need to play. They can easily amuse themselves and love to entertain others in the process. Any object of curiosity may become the center of attention for a new game, and you are almost always invited to play along. Play is an important form of exercise and a necessary outlet for pent-up energy. It is a sign of happiness and good health in all cats.

Every individual cat or group of cats will invent its own favorite cat games. Balls may be batted, kicked and chased. Any small moving object (even those that we cannot see) may be stalked, pounced on or caught. Tumbling for one, or wrestling for two; there are things to crawl under and to climb over, there is racing from room to room, jumping from sofa to chair and hurdling over other pieces of furniture. And there is always something new to be investigated. A dripping faucet is a favorite for most cats. Anything that is dark inside and can be crawled into *will* be crawled into; a paper sack, the sleeve of a jacket or the covers on the bed—all are too tempting to be avoided. The Persian's fantastic imagination and curiosity prevents it from ever growing tired of the same games.

To save on needless destruction of your favorite belongings and household objects, it helps to direct your cat's attention to safer and more appropriate toys and playthings. These toys can be purchased at local pet shops; such toys are safe to use because they're specifically designed for cats. You also can make toys yourself, and almost anything can be used. The simplest objects, such as an old shoe box (or any cardboard box), a spool

Orange-eyed white Persian. Persians show amazing concentration when they are involved in stalking.

attached to a piece of shoestring hanging from a doorknob, a small ball or a piece of aluminum foil or paper rolled into a ball, a paper bag, or best of all, a wicker basket. Of the cat toys sold at pet shops, the furry toys or cloth mice filled with catnip seem to provide the most amusement for my cats. Avoid toys with little bells that may come loose and be swallowed. Also, avoid toys with elastic strings or anything sharp that your cat might get into its mouth. Use your imagination to invent safe toys for your cat. Your cat will show you which ones are best.

SAFETY IN THE HOME

The age-old expression that "Curiosity killed the cat" are words to the wise for cat owners. A cat's curious nature will get it into all sorts of unsuspected predicaments. Some of these predicaments are funny, but others may be extremely dangerous. Cats can find themselves imprisoned in closets, cabinets and drawers; they will swallow many sorts of elastic, string (beware of tinsel from your Christmas tree!) or other small objects; they will eat or drink many types of poison if it smells or tastes pleasant enough (antifreeze is a favorite poison of outdoor cats); they will get their heads, limbs and paws caught in the most incredible places; and, last but not least, they will fall out of windows or other high places if caution is not taken to prevent it. All this is not intended to discourage or scare the potential cat owner (most young cats learn quickly to avoid dangerous situations) but is just to alert the cat owner so that accidents can be prevented before they happen. You don't need to arrange the entire house around the cat; merely

Quadruple and Triple Champion Zoda Candace of La Cresta. Bred by Zoe McEachern and owned by Betty L. Meins.

follow some of the same precautions as you would with a small child.

TRAVELING

Your Persian cat can learn to be an excellent traveling companion, especially if it learns how to travel while still young. Whether you are just driving your automobile across town or flying in a plane across the country, your Persian cat need not stay home if you would like to take it with you.

If you are planning to travel with your cat, you will need to purchase or build a cat carrier. There are many types of cat carriers which are available commercially. There are simple cardboard models which are sufficient for temporary use, and there are very sophisticated light-weight metal alloy models for the cat that wishes to travel "first-class." Of course there are a wide variety of carriers that would fall into a category between the above two types. When selecting a cat carrier, be sure that it is well ventilated and large enough for your cat to move around in. It should be well constructed so that the cat cannot claw or chew its way out, and it must have ventilation. I recommend that the carrier have a window of some sort so that the cat can look out. Some of the nicer cat carriers have clear Plexiglas tops so that the cat can see out in every direction. Most cats seem to be more comfortable when they can see where they are going. If the cat gets scared or is too nervous, you can cover the glass top or window to give the animal more privacy.

It is very easy to teach your cat to use the carrier. When you are at home, leave the carrier out with its door open and turn it into a comfortable "house" for your cat. Your

Triple Champion Gallahad's Decibel, a blue-eyed white female. Bred by Blanche Smith and owned by Don Martin.

Persian will learn to go there for protection and solitude and will eventually feel secure when in its "house." When you take the cat traveling, it will not hesitate to get into the "house" and will feel comfortable and safe during the trip.

Cats can be shipped via train, bus or plane in their

With the advances in modern shipping, many kittens are sent to their new owners from distant locations. Kittens must be properly weaned and must be old enough to leave their mother before going to their new home.

Two kittens enjoying a breather. Be sure that the carrier you purchase has adequate ventilation for your cat.

own cat carriers. To be safe, it is always a good idea to call ahead to make reservations for your cat and to get specific details about shipping. The shipper (airline, bus or train) may require a health certificate from your veterinarian showing that your pet has been recently vaccinated and is not carrying any diseases.

When making routine trips to the veterinarian, always use your cat carrier. It will protect your cat from dogs or other animals that might scare it and may help to protect it from diseases that other cats may be carrying. Your cat will always feel more comfortable in its carrier, because it will always be in the company of its "home."

Left: *Cats' claws should be clipped at least once a month. Overgrown claws can cause damage to the foot.*
Below: *The best way to keep your cat's coat beautiful and to reduce shedding is to brush the cat regularly.*

Grooming

the Persian

The Persian cat is known for its beautiful long coat and wears it with distinction. Your Persian's pride in its looks is evidenced by the long hours that it will spend preening itself with its tongue. Unfortunately, the job of grooming is too big for the Persian to handle alone. The long silky-fine coat tends to tangle and knot faster than the cat can "comb" it out with its tongue. Your Persian requires your help to look its very best.

Regular grooming is a very important part of caring for the Persian. Your Persian cat should be combed and brushed at least once a day for five to ten minutes. This is important for several reasons. Most important: your cat will look and feel better. The Persian's long hair forms tangles easily, and if these tangles are not brushed out they will rapidly grow into knots and will mat the coat badly. Mats are the scourge of longhaired cats. They are unsightly to the cat owner and irritating and even painful to the cat. Mats on a Persian, due to lack of grooming, go beyond discomfort. They can cause a breaking of the skin (sores) and lead to painful problems and expensive medical treatment. Secondly, regular grooming will help to control the shedding of cat hair onto your furniture, carpets and clothing. It is much easier to comb the dead hairs off your Persian than it is to get it out of your carpet or off your clothes. Lastly, as previously mentioned, regular grooming will help reduce the severity of hairballs. Hairballs are wads of hair that accumulate in the cat's stomach as a result of the cat's constant licking and preening to keep the coat clean.

A basic grooming kit for the Persian cat should include:

1—Stiff-bristled brush (natural bristles are best to control static electricity)

2—Combs: (Steel teeth recommended)

1—Fine (20 teeth per inch)

1—Coarse (10 teeth per inch)

Cornstarch (or other grooming powder)

Cat claw clipper

Soft-tipped cotton swabs (or cotton balls)

Make grooming your Persian cat a daily ritual. Start grooming your cat

Double Grand and Triple Champion La Cresta's Edelweiss. Bred and owned by Betty L. Meins.

Left: *Daily observation of your Persian is important. If you notice anything abnormal about your Persian's general health or behavior, call your veterinarian.* **Below and facing:** *If your Persian gets adequate exercise and play, and if you feed it a well-balanced diet and groom its coat every day, it should lead a long, healthy life.*

gently when it is very young. Kittens do not actually require as much grooming as adults, but gentle brushing with a soft-bristled brush will get them accustomed to the feeling of being groomed. The young cat will learn to think of being groomed as another way of being petted or loved. As it grows older it will look forward to the daily brushing. The grooming ritual can be a relaxing experience for you and your cat, but it must be performed every day. If you begin to miss days, the knots will be harder to comb out—and then grooming will become a chore for you and a painful experience for your cat.

Persian cats allowed to roam and roll outdoors run the risk of seriously matting their coats.

Accustom your cat to being groomed when it is very young. This way, it will come to enjoy this necessary process.

DAILY COMBING AND BRUSHING

With a little practice every Persian owner soon develops his own technique for daily grooming. I begin with the coarse-toothed steel comb first to help loosen and break up the larger snarls and tangles. I then use the fine-toothed comb to remove the smaller snarls and comb out the loose hair. The finer comb is also best for combing the shorter hairs on the face, chin and paws. Remember to comb the entire cat. Some people comb only

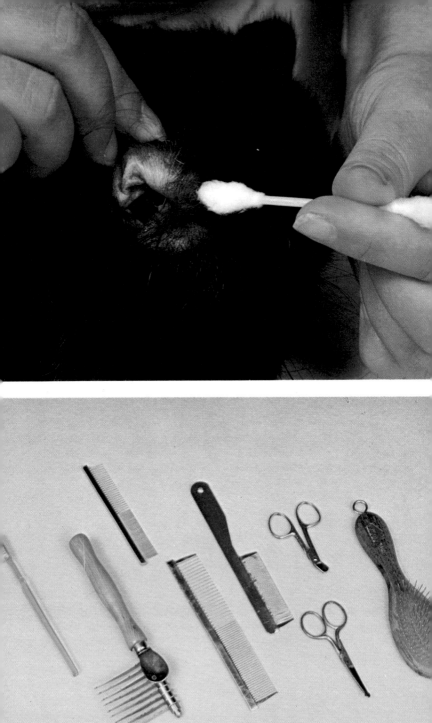

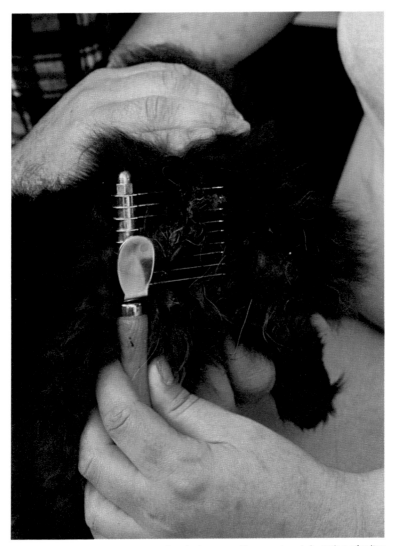

Top left: *Regular cleaning of your Persian's ears will prevent an infestation of mites. Gently wipe each ear with a soft cotton swab to remove any dirt or wax that builds up.* **Bottom left:** *Grooming is an important part of Persian care, since the Persian's long coat is too much for it to handle alone. These grooming tools will help Persian owners get the job done most efficiently, and they are available in most pet shops.* **Above:** *If you fail to thoroughly brush and comb your Persian each and every day, tangles and mats such as these will result. There are special combs for the removal of unsightly mats.*

the back and other easy-to-get-at spots, only to realize a month later that their Persian's belly is one large mat of fur. Be sure to comb the tummy, between the front and hind legs, the flanks, down the back of the hind legs (often referred to as the "pants") and under the neck. And, of course, don't forget the tail. When you think you have finished, feel the cat's entire body to check for knots or snarls you may have missed. When the cat is thoroughly combed out, use the stiff brush to brush against the natural direction of the fur. This helps to stimulate growth of new hair and gives the coat a fluffy, soft, glossy appearance. Finish the job by brushing the "ruff" (the hair around the neck) up around the head to frame the face and give the Persian a lion-like look.

REMOVAL OF MATS

If your Persian's coat has been neglected, you may find yourself having to remove mats. The problem must be fairly common, because pet shops sell products developed to help remove tangles. A good way to remove mats is to use a seam-ripper to pull apart the tightly wadded knots of dead fur. Always keep your finger in front of the sharp pointed edge of the seam-ripper; your cat will not be eager to forgive you for stabbing or scraping it. Once you have broken the mat apart into smaller knots, you can usually manage to comb them out with the coarse-toothed comb. The above method works well for smaller mats, but larger mats may become so severe that they must be clipped out. Often a trip to the veterinarian will be required.

BATHING

Even though cats are meticulously neat by their very nature, most seem to have a dislike for baths. Regular, diligent grooming

Brush the ruff up around the head to give the Persian its characteristic lionlike look.

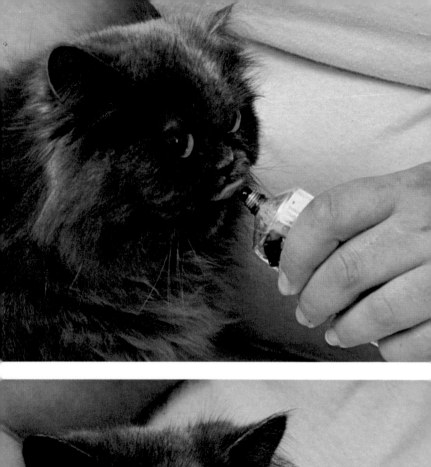

Top and bottom right: *The more hair your cat ingests as it licks itself during its personal grooming, the greater the chances are of hairballs forming in the cat's stomach. Daily brushing and an occasional bath will help remove loose hairs. Should your Persian develop hairballs, there are a number of remedies that are appealing to cats. Simply smear a small amount of the preparation on your fingertip and allow your cat to lick it off.* **Above:** *This cream tabby Persian is the picture of good health.*

of your Persian will help prevent the need for bathing. Sometimes baths are unavoidable, especially if, by some chance, your cat becomes excessively dirty. Baths are also an excellent means of getting rid of loose hair when a cat is shedding. Owners should be advised that there is no problem with bathing a cat, at any age, if it is done properly.

A dry bath sometimes can be very effective for removal of many types of grease and oily dirt. Dry shampoos of different types are commercially available at pet stores. Part the cat's fur to separate the greasy hairs and dust on the powder so that it gets down to the skin. Then brush the powder out thoroughly to remove the greasy dirt. Repeat the process until the hairs stand separately and are no longer oily. When working around the cat's head, protect its face with your hand to prevent

the powder from getting into the eyes, nose and throat.

There may be times when it may be necessary to give your pet a wet bath. Some cats will try anything to avoid getting bathed, so it is often wise to recruit another person to give you assistance. Cats are easily chilled, so it is advisable to test the water temperature to be sure that it is comfortably warm, and be sure that the room temperature is close to or over 75 degrees Fahrenheit. A large sink, bathtub or wash basin works fine for bathing a cat, but make sure you cover the bottom with a fabric (a towel, for example) that provides traction for the cat. Fill the wash basin about 4 or 5 inches deep with warm water. Carefully pick up the cat, being absolutely

Facing: *This little fellow has very prominent whiskers.*

A mother cat (like the one below, pictured in her kittening box) will do her best to groom her kittens, but once they are old enough to leave her side (like the ones pictured at left), their grooming needs must be fulfilled by their owner.

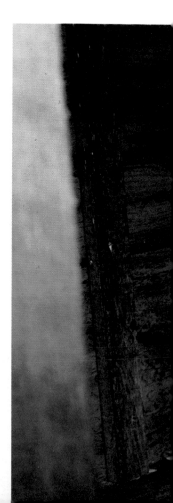

sure to support the bulk of its weight with your hand and forearm under the body, and set it in the wash basin. Some cats are very relaxed and will accept the bath water well. Other cats may make a fuss and will even try to scratch you. If this is the case, hold the cat firmly and securely, high on the scruff of the neck, and keep its back to you. This will help prevent it from biting or scratching you. Always be gentle but firm while trying to get the job done as soon as possible.

Wet the cat down, using a plastic cup to pour the water over its back. (To keep water and soap out of the cat's eyes, it helps to rub some petroleum jelly around the eyes.) Next, pour on the shampoo and work it into a lather. Use a specially made cat shampoo; don't use products designed for use on dogs or people. Be sure to wash the entire cat and to remove all grease and dirt. Rinse the cat thoroughly to remove all the shampoo.

When all the soap is rinsed off, remove the cat from the tub and quickly cover it with a large warm towel. *Do not* "rub" a cat dry; otherwise, you will have a Persian with a well knotted coat. Always "pat"

A beautifully groomed Chinchilla Persian.

dry, or blot with a good absorbent towel. Dry the cat off as much as possible with the towel and then use a hand-held hair dryer or blower to "blow-dry" the coat until it is totally dry down to the skin. Use a comb (the coarse one) to lift and separate each hair while drying. Gentle combing and drying with a dryer will create a smooth-flowing, well groomed, untangled cat. Be careful that the dryer is not so hot that it will scorch or burn the cat. The hand held dryer is an excellent tool for drying your Persian after a bath and insuring that the cat is not subject to chill or draft while damp. You should never just towel dry your Persian and then let it run

Note the clear eyes on this Persian. Before bathing, put some petroleum jelly around the cat's eyes to prevent irritation from water and soap.

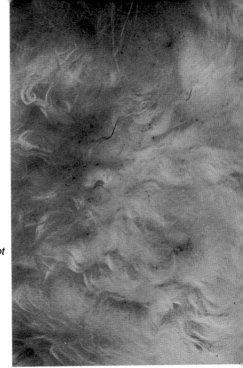

Left: *Good health and a balanced diet are essential for a beautiful, healthy Persian.* **Right:** *Close-up view of a pregnant queen's nipples. This area may become sensitive to brushing, so it may be best to hold off on grooming this area. Consult your veterinarian.* **Below:** *This is not to say, however, that the pregnant Persian doesn't need regular grooming.*

freely. Finish the job with a gentle brushing. Then give your Persian a treat for being such a good sport.

SHEDDING

Shedding of dead hair is normal for both longhaired and shorthaired cats. Longhaired cats do not shed any more than shorthaired cats; they just have longer hair that is more noticeable on furniture and clothing. Regular grooming of your Persian cat will greatly help to control this problem.

CLAWS

A cat's claws should be clipped approximately once a month, and more often, if necessary. Note that cats have five toes on their front feet and four toes on their hind feet. Be careful when clipping the claws not to clip past the pink part; this is the blood vein of the claw. Do not use human nail clippers or dog claw clippers to clip

A tortoiseshell Persian. Another way to prevent shedding on furniture is to teach your cat to stay off furniture when it is still a kitten.

beautifully groomed pair of Persians.

our cat's claws; if not
sed properly they may
ause the claws to crack.
here are specially made
lippers for your cat which

are excellent for this
purpose. Ask your pet
dealer or veterinarian for a
demonstration on how to
clip your cat's claws.

Left: Young kittens should learn early what the scratching post is for; otherwise they will seek an alternative such as your furniture, draperies, or carpeting. **Right:** If you have purchased a kitten that has been properly weaned from its mother, it should already be trained to the litter box. **Below:** It is important to provide your Persian kitten with a comfortable place to sleep. A wicker basket with a soft, cushiony pillow will suffice.

Feeding the Persian

NUTRITIONAL NEEDS AND EATING BEHAVIOR

Good nutrition is extremely important to the health and well-being of your Persian cat. Like the wild cats which are its ancestors, the domesticated Persian cat is a true carnivore (meat eater) and as such has a definite need for animal sources of protein and fat. Pure animal or fish meat alone, though, is not sufficient to meet your cat's nutritional needs. Wild cats that must hunt for survival will tend to eat animals that eat vegetables or grain. Only

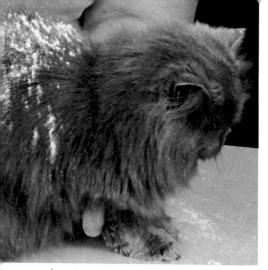

Left: *Grooming will maintain your cat, but nutrition will make him beautiful in the first place.* **Below:** *Colorful ribbons and awards line the walls of Mrs. Marianne Lawrence's Insta-Purr Cattery.*

by devouring its prey whole, including the bones, organs, skin and whatever greenery its prey may have eaten, is the wild cat able to meet all of its nutritional needs.

Cats require a special type of protein in their diets, and they require a much larger amount of protein than most other animals. In fact, cats need more than twice the protein and B-vitamins that dogs need. Cats also have a high requirement for fats, most of which must be animal fat. If a cat's diet is too low in protein, fats and essential vitamins, it is likely to lose its appetite and develop a dry and lusterless coat, and it may

even encounter more serious health problems.

Aside from the cat's unique nutritional needs, it also has its own distinctive eating behavior. Cats have a very keen sense of taste and smell and for this reason are very discriminatory about the food they eat. Cats are actually not finicky by nature, but they may become so if given too great a selection of foods to eat. Cats are occasional eaters; unlike dogs, which like to gorge a meal all at

one time, cats will prefer to nibble smaller quantities of food at different times during the day and night. A final observation is that the cat is an uninhibited eater. When it decides it is ready to eat, there is very little that can distract it from enjoying its meal.

If you think all of this sounds rather complex, you're right. The cat is a very complex animal, nutritionally, and there is still very much to be known in this regard. Still, feeding your cat can be a very simple task if you follow a few basic guidelines and use common sense.

TYPES OF CAT RATIONS
In general, there is really only one type of food to feed to your cat: commercial cat foods. In theory, homemade cat foods can be excellent if they are formulated so that they are well balanced nutritionally. In practice, however, making up your own homemade cat food

can be a very complex task, and for this reason I would suggest it only for the most experienced cat owners. An unbalanced homemade diet can lead to serious health problems for your cat.

Today's commercial cat foods are a safe bet for meeting the nutritional requirements of your cat. If you are planning to feed a commercial cat ration as a steady diet, be sure to read the label on the package or can. If the label states that the cat food is "balanced, perfect, complete, scientific or adequate for all cats," you can be assured that the ration is sufficient to meet all the nutritional needs of your kitten (for growth) or adult cat. Some commercial cat foods are adequate only for the adult cat, and others should be used only as supplements or special treats to enhance the flavor of your cat's regular ration.

Some pet shops sell

In the wild, cats received a diet containing the necessary proteins, vitamins, and minerals. It is up to the owner of the domesticated cat to provide the same nutrients for his pet.

The Persian has been among the most popular feline breeds for many years. The Persian's pleasant disposition and lovely expression have found it many admirers.

specially formulated cat foods that are nutritionally complete and meet the dietary requirements of *all* cats. Such foods may be slightly more expensive than those sold in grocery outlets, but they can be well worth the extra cost.

The commercial brands of cat food are available in three forms: dry, soft-moist and moist (or canned). Dry cat foods are better for your cat's teeth and can be left out all the time for your cat to nibble on as it pleases. This is a convenient way to feed your cat, and most cats will eat dry cat food without complaints. A word of caution: Dry food *should not* be fed as the sole diet for your cat. Cats need the nutrient found in wet foods as well. A cat, like any other human or animal, requires variety and a well-rounded diet. When using dry food for male cats, in particular, select the one with the *lowest* ash content to aid

in prevention of FUS, a deadly and fast disease common with the male cat. (Feline Urinary Syndrome causes a "blockage" of the urinary tract leading to a painful death. If you see your cat going to the litter box often, straining, with no results, get it to the veterinarian fast.) Moist cat foods, on the other hand, appear to be slightly more flavorful to most cats (and most owners of finicky cats prefer it for their cats for this reason), however, if moist cat foods are fed as the sole diet, the cat will accumulate more tartar on the teeth, which will increase the chances of gum and teeth disease. Moist cat food also will spoil if left out for long periods of time. The soft-moist types of cat food are a compromise between the dry and moist types of rations. The soft-moist cat foods can contain more protein (and for this reason are more flavorful) than the dry cat foods, and

A beautiful calico Persian. Top Persian breeders have developed healthy feline diets through trial and error. As each cat is an individual, find out what your pet's likes and dislikes are and tailor his feeding program accordingly. Do remember, however, that variety and nutrition are paramount to a good diet.

Cats have preferences just like people do, so be sure not to spoil your pet by overfeeding his particular favorite.

they can be left out for your cat to eat at its convenience; on the other hand, they will not prevent the build-up of tartar on your cat's teeth.

Cats love and need variety in their diet. It is unwise to feed your Persian only one type or flavor of food (such as liver only, or chicken only, etc.) because the cat may become addicted to it to the point that it will eat nothing else, and that one food may not meet all nutritional requirements. Fortunately, there is a great selection of brands and flavors of cat food available today. Your cat will love to test them for you and will tell you which ones it likes best. Cats are individuals and in many respects are like people in their discriminatory eating behavior. You may find that your cat loves the chicken-flavor cat food one week and will absolutely refuse to eat it the next. This is perfectly normal—

but you should be careful of overcatering to feline whims or your cat may become finicky about what it eats.

As a general recommendation for feeding older kittens and adult cats, I suggest that a good-quality nutritionally "complete" commercial dry cat food be left out at all times. This allows your cat to pick and nibble at its leisure, as cats (and especially Persians) like to do. Cats love to nibble

Cats and dogs can be good friends, but they should not be fed the same food, as they have different nutritional requirements.

between naps and playtime and most of all seem to look forward to their middle-of-the-night snack. Most cats will eat only as much as their bodies require to maintain optimum condition. A small percentage of cats may tend to overeat; if your Persian is in this group, the cat should not be allowed to self-feed in this manner. If you do decide to leave dry food out at all times, I suggest that you also feed your cat a small amount of canned or soft-moist cat food once or even twice a day to provide it with the variety of foods it needs and will enjoy.

The amount to feed your cat will vary with its age, sex, size and individual metabolism. Every cat is different with regard to the types of food it prefers and the amount of food it consumes. Each owner must observe his or her cat to know how much the animal should eat. The best way to go about this is to observe the fitness of your cat. If you cannot feel your cat's ribs, then your cat is too fat and you are feeding too much. A good rule of thumb is that you should be able to feel the ribs, yet there should be a fair amount of muscle on them.

If you do not wish to leave dry food out for your cat, you should feed nutritionally balanced ration at least two times a day. Kittens should be fed at least three or four times a day. If your kitten or cat is eating all that you are providing and it still looks underweight, you should increase the size of each serving.

WATER

Be sure that your cat or kitten has plenty of fresh, clean water available at ALL times. Even though cats are "arid" creatures by nature and are able to go for fairly long periods of time without water if

Headstudy of a Chinchilla Persian.

necessary, it is very important that your cat always has fresh, clean water available.

VITAMINS
Although supplementing the cat's diet is usually not necessary if the cat is receiving and eating a good, nutritionally complete commercial cat food, certain vitamin supplements, such as those containing vitamins B, C and E and additional protein, are not harmful and may be of benefit in certain cases. Be careful to avoid over-supplementation with

vitamins A and D and calcium and phosphorus.

FEEDING MILK
Milk is an excellent food for growing kittens and for the adult mother cat during pregnancy and lactation. Unfortunately, most cats have difficulty digesting milk and will get diarrhea. For this reason, it is best that milk not be fed after the kitten has passed the nursing age (between two to three months, depending on when the mother cat decides it is time for the kittens to become independent).

The Healthy Persian

When you purchase a new Persian cat or kitten, regardless of the source, it should already have been vaccinated and it should be accompanied by some type of health guarantee that it is free of disease at the time of purchase. If, for some reason, your new Persian has *not* had its shots, make an appointment to see your veterinarian immediately. He will examine the animal for any signs of disease and will most likely suggest that it be vaccinated for feline distemper (also called panleukopenia or feline infectious enteritis) and possibly rabies. There are also vaccines available for several upper respiratory diseases that affect kittens and cats. These inoculations are the cheapest and most effective form of insurance for the protection of your cat's health.

FINDING THE RIGHT VETERINARIAN

The future of your cat's health and someday even your cat's life may depend on your veterinarian. With this in mind, it is important to choose a veterinarian who is well qualified and with whom you feel comfortable. To become a veterinarian requires many years of hard work and a love for animals, but not all veterinarians will necessarily be equally sympathetic to the needs of you and your cat.

To locate a veterinarian, ask other cat owners or breeders who they consult when their pet becomes ill. Word of mouth is the veterinarian's best (or worst) form of advertisement, depending on how conscientious he is. Other cat owners will have had previous firsthand experience with a veterinarian.

Before going to see the veterinarian for the first time, make a list of any questions you may have concerning the health of your cat or kitten. When

If you keep more than one kitten, make sure they both get enough food, as some kittens mature faster and may become little bullies.

you enter the veterinarian's office, begin making mental notes and ask yourself a few questions: Is the office neat, clean and orderly? Is the receptionist (or veterinary assistant) pleasant and neat in appearance? Observe the veterinarian as he handles your cat. Does he seem to like cats? The veterinarian should show confidence and compassion in the way he handles your cat, being gentle yet firm. A good veterinarian will begin by asking your cat's name and talking gently to the animal. Next, he will want to take notes about your cat's medical history. Do not be afraid to interview the veterinarian. A good veterinarian will be glad to tell you why he is qualified to care for your cat. If he appears impatient with you or your cat, if he is unwilling to answer all of your questions in a manner that you can clearly understand, or if he is unwilling to discuss his fees before he treats your cat, go to another veterinarian.

HOW TO TELL WHETHER YOUR CAT IS SICK

Routine daily observation of your cat is a good way to detect any early signs of disease. In other words, GET TO KNOW YOUR CAT! Any sudden change in the cat's normal behavior could be an indication that it may not be feeling well. This is not to say that any change in the cat's behavior means that it is sick; cats can be moody at times. But if you are in doubt for any reason, always call your veterinarian.

If your cat develops any of the following symptoms, make an appointment to see your veterinarian as soon as possible:

—Loss of appetite for more than three days in a row

—Repeated vomiting

—Repeated diarrhea

Blue-and-white bicolor Persian.

—Blood in the urine or stool

—Dullness of the haircoat with excessive shedding or hair loss which leaves bare patches

—Straining to urinate (or showing signs of difficult or painful urination or defecation, or spending long or repeated periods in the litter box without results)

—Dehydration or reluctance to drink water

—Excessive, constant thirst

—Red watery eyes, or yellow dull-looking eyes

—Reluctance to move

—Acute swelling or lumps anywhere on the body

—Runny nose

—Persistent coughing or sneezing for more than two days

—A "drunken" or "dizzy" attitude

—Fever: A rectal temperature of greater than 102°F.

COMMON DISEASES AND AILMENTS

FELINE INFECTIOUS ENTERITIS (also called feline distemper or feline panleukopenia): This deadly viral disease can be passed from one cat to another. Signs of this disease are high fever, depression, weight loss, dehydration, vomiting, diarrhea and intensive thirst. Any, all or none of the above signs may be seen. At present, the only way to stop this disease is to prevent it before it occurs. This is why it is very important to vaccinate kittens for feline enteritis when they are still young. Your veterinarian can determine the age at which to administer this vaccine to your new kitten. Cats should also receive a booster shot every year. Special blood tests are often necessary to diagnose this disease accurately. If your veterinarian has confirmed that your cat has this disease, warn owners of other cats that may have been in contact with yours. Be sure that other cats in the household are vaccinated, and disinfect the cat's bed, litter box, and food and water dishes with a household antiseptic. Do not bring another cat into the house for at least three months.

RABIES: Rabies is one of the oldest and deadliest of diseases of animals and man. Fortunately, today it is rare among domestic cats. Cases of rabies were known to have occurred as early as the 23rd century B.C. Rabies is a highly

A calico Persian owned by Jose Langevin.

contagious disease and can be spread from animal to animal as well as from animal to man. At different times, in certain areas of the country, rabies may be carried by bats, skunks and other species of wildlife. If there is the slightest risk that your cat may be exposed to rabies, it should be vaccinated. The rabies virus affects the nervous system, and animals with this disease may appear abnormally aggressive ("mad") or wild animals may sometimes appear unusually tame ("dumb").

UPPER RESPIRATORY DISEASE VIRUSES (also called FVR or Feline Viral Rhinotracheitis): This disease is a type of "cold" that affects kittens and cats. In some cases, kittens may catch this "cold" when they are very young and may have the disease the rest of their lives. This chronic, long-lasting cold can make some cats miserable for many years. Some of them may "carry" the disease and thus may infect other cats, even though they may not be affected themselves. The disease is contagious only between cats. Symptoms are: depression, loss of appetite, sneezing, discharge from the eyes and nose and sores in the mouth.

FIP-FELINE INFECTIOUS PERITONITIS: This disease is now recognized as one of the major deadly diseases of cats. FIP is a viral disease and can be passed from cat to cat. Some cats will show no obvious symptoms as the disease progresses. Others will show signs of fever, depression, loss of appetite or weight loss. At this time, the best way to prevent this disease is to prevent exposure to free-roaming cats.

Internal Parasites
Three of the major internal

A black Persian. Note the beautiful copper eyes.

parasites of cats are hookworms, tapeworms and roundworms. Your veterinarian can tell whether your cat has these parasites by observing a specimen of its stool under the microscope.

TAPEWORMS—If you see small, creamy-white "rice-like" segments around your cat's anal region or on the tail, you may be looking at tapeworms. These small segments release eggs that are eaten by fleas. When the cat licks its fur, and in so doing swallows the fleas, the worms are released into the digestive tract of the cat. Therefore, the best way to prevent tapeworms is to keep your cat (and its living quarters) free of fleas.

HOOKWORMS—These blood-sucking parasites can be especially detrimental to young kittens. They are called hookworms because of the hook-like teeth they use to attach themselves to the intestinal tract of the animal. Hookworms are most commonly found in geographic locations where the climate is warm the year 'round.

ROUNDWORMS (also called ascarids)—Roundworms are probably the most common intestinal parasites of cats. If the mother cat is infected she can pass the worms on to her kittens. In advanced cases of roundworm infestation, cats may experience bouts of coughing and may have a fever. Kittens and cats may have a pot-bellied appearance and appear listless.

In general, cats with internal parasites will have a dull coat and can experience a weight loss even though they have an increased appetite; additionally, there may be coughing, vomiting or diarrhea. See your veterinarian for an accurate diagnosis. Most parasitic infestations can be treated effectively if caught in time.

External Parasites
FLEAS—Fleas are blood-feeders that affect cats, dogs, man and many other animals. Aside from the severe discomfort, a result of the constant itching they cause, fleas can also carry other diseases. In some cases the itching may be so severe that cats may scratch themselves until they are bloody. To prevent fleas, use a flea collar or a flea powder made especially for cats. (Be sure to check the label of the product you purchase to insure it is safe to use on your Persian. Pet shops carry a

Champion Bre-Etta Perfecto, a blue male. Bred and owned by Mary Ann Maxwell.

full line of flea collars and powders and sprays.) If your cat has fleas, the veterinarian can prescribe a special shampoo to remove them. Be sure to de-flea the cat outside and to clean the house and the cat's bedding thoroughly to remove the flea eggs.

LICE—Lice are less common than fleas. They are also smaller than fleas, so they are harder to detect with the naked eye. Lice will cause severe irritation and itching and will cause cats to scratch themselves. Some flea powders and shampoos will kill lice, but it is best to ask your veterinarian or pet dealer for a specific recommendation.

TICKS—Ticks may be found occasionally on cats that are allowed outdoors. They are brown, hard-shelled parasites that bury their head under the skin and suck blood. If you find a tick on your cat, often it can be removed by simply pulling it off the cat with steady tension. If the head of the tick breaks off and remains imbedded in the skin, see your veterinarian.

EAR MITES—Dirt and wax in the cat's ears is a breeding ground for ear mites. These parasites will form little brown scabs that may look like dark brown dirt. Symptoms of ear mites are constant scratching of the ears and continual head shaking. See your veterinarian for accurate diagnosis and treatment.

Skin Diseases

RINGWORM—This disease of the skin causes round to oval bare patches to appear in the coat, usually around the area of the head. Ringworm is not caused by a worm but is instead a fungal disease. It can be transmitted from cat to cat—and to people—by direct contact.

ALLERGIC DERMATITIS—It is now being recognized by veterinarians that many of the skin diseases of cats are actually caused by allergic reactions to fleas, certain types of food and a large variety of other things. These skin diseases may be very difficult to treat in some cases.

MANGE—This disease is caused by mites that burrow into the cat's skin and cause excessive hair loss. The form of mange most commonly seen in cats will often cause bare spots around the eyes.

Other Ailments

HAIRBALLS—Hairballs are wads of hair that accumulate in the cat's stomach as a result of its constant licking and cleaning with the tongue. Persian cats are more prone to getting hairballs because of the increased amount of hair they swallow. Remember that daily grooming on the part of the Persian owner is the most effective preventive measure against the problem of hairballs. Should you need them, the products sold in pet shops specifically to help in hairball removal are the quite effective remedies.

VOMITING AND DIARRHEA—These two problems are not actually

Dearheart Fantasia, a Chinchilla female. Bred and owned by Dr. and Mrs. P.N. Ramsdale.

diseases, but are instead symptoms of many diseases. Mild transitory diarrhea or vomiting may be seen in kittens or young cats as a result of a change in diet or mild digestive upset. These can often be treated effectively with certain human remedies such as Kaolin or Kaopectate. Check with your veterinarian to find out how much to give your cat or kitten. In some cases, feeding a little cottage cheese may help to clear up diarrhea; otherwise, do not give the cat food for 12 hours. This will allow the cat's stomach time to settle down. If vomiting or diarrhea persists, see your veterinarian.

FEVER—Fever is a sign of infection, inflammation or disease. Heat stroke and other problems also can cause a fever. In any case, fever is a sign of potential serious disease, so be sure to contact your veterinarian.

Fever is detected by taking the cat's temperature with a rectal thermometer. Lubricate the thermometer with petroleum jelly and gently insert it in the cat's rectum about 1 to 1½ inches. Hold the thermometer in the rectum for at least one minute. Normal temperature for the cat is 100° to 102°F. Above 102°F is considered a fever.

UROLITHIASIS— Urolithiasis is the formation of stones in the bladder or urethra. The exact cause of this disease is not fully understood; however male cats are more severely affected than females. Since the male has a longer and narrower urethra, stones are more likely to become lodged and cause a blockage. Female cats will show signs of frequent urination. Male cats will have signs of straining to urinate, painful urination or straining with no results. If your cat is showing any of these symptoms, see your veterinarian *immediately*. Total blockage of the urethra, incidentally, can cause death . . . overnight.

PREVENTING DISEASE IN YOUR CAT

Prevention is always the best medicine for any disease. There are many diseases of cats, especially the viral diseases, which are very difficult to cure but can be easily prevented. In some cases, death is the final outcome of these diseases. This is why vaccines are your veterinarian's most powerful medicine.

To maintain the good health of your cat and protect it from potential harm:

(1) Vaccinate kittens as soon as they are weaned from their mother. This is important, since after the kittens stop nursing, they no longer receive those antibodies through their mother's milk to help fight disease and infection. Vaccines are available for feline enteritis (distemper), rabies and upper respiratory disease

The best way to prevent illness at an early stage is to know your cat. If you are familiar with your cat's habits and idiosyncracies, you are more likely to notice when something is wrong.

viruses. See your veterinarian for his recommendation; he can tell you at what age you should have your kitten vaccinated. Your cat should also have a booster shot and a complete examination at least once a year.

(2) Feed your cat a balanced, nutritionally complete diet.

(3) Know your cat and watch for signs of disease.

(4) Prevent your cat from roaming freely outdoors. Stray cats carry diseases that can infect your pet. Your cat can also get into fights with other animals, and scratches and bites can easily become infected—and don't forget that cars are one of the biggest killers of cats. Protect your precious Persian by keeping your pet safely indoors.

The breeding of purebred Persian cats is a very complex and specialized field. It requires serious planning and thought, special care, a knowledge of the science of genetics and a true love for the Persian breed. It is not, therefore, a task to be undertaken by the inexperienced amateur.

If you own a purebred Persian and are considering breeding him or her, contact an experienced breeder for details and assistance. The breeder will help you locate a stud for your queen or will help to establish your registered tom as a Persian "up for stud." The breeder also can provide valuable information concerning family traits and how to make genetic crosses that will improve the breed.

WHEN TO BREED

Cats begin to feel sexual drives at a fairly early age, usually at about an age of eight to nine months;

females tend to mature slightly earlier. It is not recommended to breed the female before ten months of age, because if she becomes pregnant before this time, she may not develop fully herself.

Prior to breeding, be sure that your queen (sexually mature female cat) is in good general health. Take her to your veterinarian for a complete examination. She should be free of all internal and external parasites and be in a good nutritional state (not too fat or too thin). She should be given a booster vaccination at this time so that she will have good immunity to disease to pass on to her kittens.

The fully mature female cat will have a tendency to come into "season" normally during the spring and fall; it is feasible, however, for a queen to come into season at *any* time of the year. This is the breeding season, during which time the queen is

A blue Persian.

sexually active. The queen's sexual activity is controlled at least partly by the length of days. Early spring to late fall is the time of the year during which the days are longest. The queen will "come into heat" during this time.

"Heat" is when the female cat will allow the male tom to mate with her. Only if bred during "heat" (estrus) can a cat become pregnant. During the breeding season, the queen will usually come into heat (estrus) approximately every 14 to 21 days and remain in heat for a minimum of four days (usually more than four is common) unless she is bred. The actual length of the heat period will vary depending on the individual cat and geographic location. Some queens may appear to remain in "heat" constantly during the mating season if they are not bred. Individual queens vary greatly as to the incidence of their heat periods; some are in heat much more frequently than others.

If you plan to breed your queen to a stud (owned by a breeder), all arrangements for breeding should be made well in advance of when the female is expected to go into heat. This way the breeder, and the male cat, will be well prepared for the arrival of the female. (It is customary for the queen to mate with the male on *his* territory, not hers!) The queen should be taken to the male at the first sign of "calling." "Calling" is increased vocalization by the female and is an early sign of heat. Other signs of heat are: an unusual display of affection (such as constantly rubbing against one's legs); continuous rolling as though she is "dizzy"; and assumption, when being petted, of a crouching position, with her hind quarters elevated, kneading and treading with her hind limbs. The female should be bred by the male during this time.

After mating occurs with the arranged sire, it is important that the female be kept indoors and not be exposed to other male cats. Female cats can remain in heat even after being bred, and, if mated by another male, may have litters of mixed parentage.

PREGNANCY AND DELIVERY

The normal length of pregnancy in cats is approximately 60 to 65 days. During this time, the expectant mother will go on with life as usual. As she approaches full term, she will be eating more each week, since she will need extra energy and protein for her kittens to grow. By the third or fourth week of pregnancy, your veterinarian should be able to feel the kittens and in some cases may be able to tell you how many are on the way. During the last week of pregnancy, the expectant mother will become restless and start

Champion Elco's Tiny Tim of Angelita, a red tabby peke-faced male. Bred by Ella Conroy and owned by Pauline Frankenfield.

to look for a secluded, quiet place to have her kittens. At this time, the queen should be made familiar with the maternity (or kittening) box.

A maternity box can be constructed out of any cardboard box of suitable size. The box should be large enough for the mother to stretch out with her kittens and still have extra room. The sides of the box should be high enough so that the mother cat can get in and the kittens cannot get out. Line the bottom of the box with newspapers and an old carpet or blanket (preferably one that can be washed). This will allow the queen to build a comfortable nest for her kittens. Put the maternity box in a quiet and private area of the house where it is warm and dry. The top of the maternity box should be covered so that it is dark and private inside, but the cover should be easily removable to allow access to the mother and kittens.

Most pet Persian queens will prefer that you be with

them prior to and while they are having their kittens. Others may seek complete privacy, and privacy should be permitted in such cases. In any case, it is a good idea to be close by to offer assistance if it is needed.

During the labor period, do not insist that the queen stay in the maternity box. In between labor pains, she may be restless and thirsty, and she may decide to get up and walk around. This is normal behavior. She will return to the box when she feels ready. If she has severe contractions for more than two hours and no kittens have appeared, call your veterinarian immediately for assistance. Persian kittens have larger bones than most kittens, and a veterinarian's help is sometimes necessary to insure a safe delivery.

The birth of four kittens will usually take about two or three hours. The kittens, each attached to its

placenta by an umbilical cord, will arrive covered with a thin transparent membrane. The mother will usually lick this off the kitten, but if she does not, be sure to remove it yourself so that the kitten can breathe (do not offer assistance unless it is necessary). Each placenta (afterbirth) is attached to the umbilical cord, and it will be expelled from the mother. The mother will then cut the umbilical cord with her teeth and eat the afterbirth (one is usually sufficient). Do not interfere with the queen as she does this.

For the first three days after delivery, allow the mother and her babies as much privacy as possible. DO NOT ALLOW VISITORS, AND DO NOT HANDLE THE KITTENS. The mother will clean up her box and make it comfortable for her and for the kittens.

Kittens are born blind and usually will not open

Newly independent kittens are quite small, but it must be remembered that they are growing at a very fast rate and that they need almost as much food as adult cats.

their eyes for seven to ten days. Keep the lights low to give their eyes time to adjust.

The kittens should begin to nurse soon after birth.

To feed her kittens, the mother will need extra energy, so be sure she is eating a good quality cat food that is nutritionally balanced for growth and lactation, and allow her to eat all she desires. It is important that each kitten receive adequate milk. Most kitten deaths are caused by a lack of milk and occur during the first week of life. Check each of the kittens to be sure that they are all getting their share. You will know whether the kittens are hungry; hungry kittens will be restless and will whine and mew constantly. If the mother is not producing enough milk, she may not be getting enough to eat. If she appears to be eating plenty of canned or soft-moist cat food and still seems to not be producing enough milk, consult your veterinarian.

If it becomes necessary to feed the kittens by hand, you can feed them a commercially prepared milk replacer. These are available from your pet store or veterinarian. Give the milk replacer, according to directions, with an eye dropper every two or three hours. A good homemade milk replacer can be made by mixing two cups of milk, one teaspoon corn syrup, the yolk of an egg and a pinch of salt. (If the kittens have loose stools, reduce the amount of corn syrup).

Sometime between the age of two and three months, the queen will decide to wean her kittens. Gradually, she will refuse to allow her kittens to nurse, and her milk supply will begin to diminish naturally. During this time, you should begin to feed the kittens a commercially prepared cereal product to start weaning them away from their mother's milk. To get them started, it may help to mix the cereal with a little milk (enough to make it mushy) and smear it on their lips. When they lick it off, they will begin to get accustomed to the new taste and will eventually grow to like it. After two to three weeks of this, they can start being weaned

An assortment of Persian color varieties.

onto canned foods. When a kitten is about two months old, it should be completely independent of its mother and should be given plenty of nourishing food. Newly independent cats eat about as much as fully adult cats.

The one thing you should never do is to breed your female without first having given some serious thought to the question of disposing of the young.

You should not have a hard time finding good homes for Persian kittens. Often times, they may all be spoken for soon after they are born. Your veterinarian or pet shop owner also may be able to help you find people who are interested in owning a beautiful Persian. But sometimes you won't have any ready takers for the kittens, which is a bad situation for everybody. Make sure you know where the kittens are to go *before* your Persian is bred.

A Little About Cat Shows

Every cat show is structured differently, but in general they are structured so that your cat will compete (at least initially) against other cats of the same breed, color, sex and show category. Most shows have three major categories: championship classes for adult whole cats (sometimes called show classes), championship alter classes, and non-championship kitten classes. Championship classes in shows are for both "whole" and "altered" cats. Both of these categories are considered championship and cats compete to earn the titles of champion or grand champion. Different associations do have different terms such as "championship" (whole cats) and "premiership" (altered cats) to describe classes, with corresponding titles, i.e., grand champion, altered grand champion or premier grand champion.

Various cat fancier magazines, organizations and clubs provide information concerning upcoming shows. To enter your cat in the show in which you wish it to compete, all you need do is to fill out an entry form.

Cat shows are for everybody. Whether your cat is a registered, pedigreed Persian champion or just a household pet and companion, many cat shows will have classes in which your cat is eligible to compete. Cat shows are highly competitive, but they can be lots of fun.

Index

PERSIAN CATS
KW-061